What Is the Engineering Process?

HOUGHTON MIFFLIN HARCOURT

PHOTOGRAPHY CREDITS: COVER (bg) ©Corbis; 3 (t) ©Comstock/Getty Images; 4 (l) ©Stockbyte/Getty Images; 4 (c) Photodisc/Getty Images; 4 (r) ©graficart.net/Alamy Images; 5 (t) ©Photodisc/Getty Images; 6 (b) ©Science & Society Picture Library/SSPL/Getty Images; 7 (t) ©Underwood & Underwood/Corbis; 8 ©Bettmann/Corbis; 9 (b) ©Mary Evans Picture Library/Photo Researchers, Inc.; 10 (t) ©Library of Congress Prints & Photographs Division; 11 ©Library of Congress Prints & Photographs Division; 12 (b) ©Library of Congress; 13 (b) ©Paul Giamou/Aurora Photos/Corbis; 14 (b) ©Bettmann/Corbis; 15 (t) ©Hirz/Getty Images; 15 (c) ©Corbis; 15 (b) ©Corbis; 16 (b) ©Roc Canals Photography/Getty Images; 19 (b) ©Corbis; 20 (b) ©Don Farrall/Getty Images; 21 (b) ©PhotoDisc/Getty Images; 22 (b) ©Maximilian Stock Ltd./Stone/Getty Images

Printed in Mexico

ISBN: 978-0-544-07302-9

4 5 6 7 8 9 10 0908 21 20 19 18 17 16

4500608014   A B C D E F G

Be an Active Reader!

 Look for each word in yellow along with its meaning.

tool   engineering

technology   prototype

design   advertisement

 <u>Underlined</u> **sentences answer these questions.**

How can technology improve products we use every day?

How can technology solve problems?

What is technology?

How can technology make dreams come true?

What is the first step of the design process?

What are the second and third steps of the design process?

What happens during the fourth step of the design process?

What is the fifth step of the design process?

Do all engineers use a design process?

What is a designed system?

What is a technological system?

How can the design process help you?

How do you complete the design process?

How can technology improve products we use every day?

Technology can improve products we use every day by making them easier to use. Technology can also make products safer or cheaper. About 100 years ago, milk only came in glass bottles. The bottles were very heavy and hard to transport. They could be reused but it cost a lot of money to make them.

Around 80 years ago, companies started making paper cartons, or boxes, for milk. The paper cartons were not as heavy as glass bottles. They were also cheaper to make than glass bottles. But the cartons were not very strong. Milk sometimes leaked out.

About 60 years ago, someone made the first plastic milk container. Plastic is stronger than paper. It is not heavy, like glass. Large bottles could be made with handles. This made pouring the milk easier. We still use all three kinds of milk containers today. Which do you think is best?

glass bottle

paper carton

plastic jug

How can technology solve problems?

A tool is any object that people use to make or do something. A pencil is a tool used to make marks for writing or drawing. Pencils were first made of wood. Inside the wood was a core called a lead. Pencil leads are actually not made of lead, but graphite. This is the part that makes marks. You have to sharpen a wooden pencil often when you are writing, so pencils wear down. Sometimes they break.

Technology can solve problems by improving on designs and materials. Someone invented a mechanical pencil to solve the problem of pencils wearing down and breaking. The outside tube of a mechanical pencil is made of plastic or metal. Thin pieces of graphite fit inside the tube. The mechanical pencil never has to be sharpened.

Today we need a new kind of pencil. You can't use a pencil on a computer touch screen. The solution is a stylus. A stylus is made of plastic and can't scratch the touch screen.

Which tools do you use to write or draw?

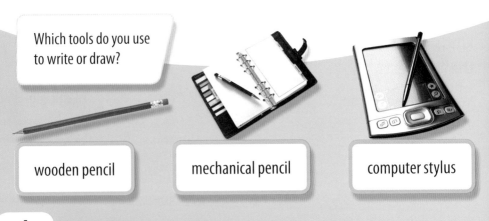

wooden pencil

mechanical pencil

computer stylus

People use technology every day. What types of technology do you use?

What is technology?

Changes to milk containers and pencils were possible because of technology. Technology is any designed system, product, or process that people use to solve problems. Technology can help us improve things that already exist. It can also help us make brand-new things that we want or need.

You might think that technology is just computers or other electronic devices. You might also think that all technology needs to run on electricity. But this is not true. Simple technology, such as pencils and milk cartons, is all around us. In fact, there is more simple technology in everyday life than advanced technology.

How can technology make dreams come true?

Have you ever wanted to fly like a bird? People had this dream for many years.

Leonardo da Vinci was an artist and scientist. He thought there was a way that people could fly. Around 1488, he drew pictures of flying machines. But Leonardo could not build his flying machines. He did not have the right technology.

Technology improved. In 1783, people flew the first hot air balloon. In 1848, the first wooden gliders flew through the air in Europe. People could ride in the gliders. These gliders didn't have engines, though. They could not fly far or go too high in the air. But they were a start. Every improvement brought the dream of flight closer to reality. Improvements in technology can make things possible that were once thought impossible.

Otto Lilienthal made 2,000 glider flights in the 1890s.

The Wright brothers started out selling and repairing bicycles at their own shop.

What is the first step of the design process?

Brothers Wilbur and Orville Wright lived in Ohio in the late 1800s and owned their own bicycle shop. They read about the glider flights in Europe. In 1898, they decided to make and fly their own flying machine.

The brothers used a design process to make their goal a reality. To design means to imagine something and prepare plans and drawings so that it can be built. A process is a series of steps that occur in a certain order.

The first step in the design process is identifying a problem. The Wright brothers saw a need for something that was better than a glider. They wanted to make an airplane that a person could control. The airplane needed an engine so that it could fly a long distance.

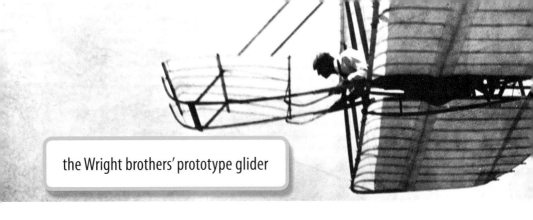

the Wright brothers' prototype glider

What are the second and third steps of the design process?

The second step of the design process is to plan and build. Wilbur and Orville made a plan. They learned more about engineering. Engineering is a way of using scientific and mathematical knowledge to develop something practical. The brothers wrote to other engineers who were also studying flight. All the engineers shared their knowledge.

The brothers made observations. They watched birds fly and talked about how the birds' wings worked. They made a kite to test some of their ideas. They took notes and made drawings.

At last the brothers felt they had gathered enough information. They were ready to build a wooden prototype glider. A prototype is a model on which something is based.

If a prototype works, the actual product can be made. Otherwise, a new and improved prototype will be built and tested.

The third step of the design process is testing the prototype. The prototype is the solution to the problem. However, it may not be the right solution! Wilbur and Orville needed a windy place to test their prototype. They moved to Kitty Hawk, North Carolina.

The first test was a success! Wilbur and Orville improved the prototype. They made more flights. They wrote notes about the flights. Often, they took pictures and studied them.

Wilbur and Orville still wanted a better prototype. The brothers moved on to the fourth step in the design process.

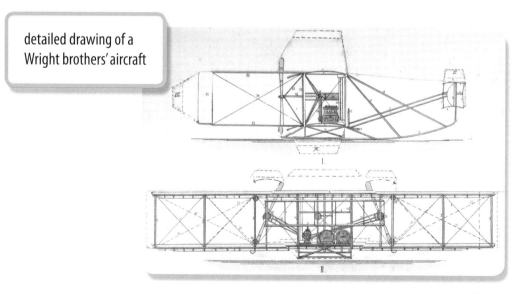

detailed drawing of a
Wright brothers' aircraft

The Wright brothers made many changes to their prototype.

What happens during the fourth step of the design process?

The fourth step in the design process is redesigning the solution or prototype. Wilbur and Orville designed and built a wind tunnel. A wind tunnel is a building with a large fan that creates a strong wind. They tested their gliders in this wind tunnel. They used what they discovered to redesign their prototype. The new, improved prototype worked well.

The prototype needed an engine, so Wilbur and Orville built one. The plane also needed a propeller. The brothers built that, too. It was time to test the new airplane. Wilbur and Orville were sure the airplane would fly. They even named it the *Flyer*. The first few times, though, the airplane would not fly. So, the brothers made more changes to the *Flyer*.

On December 17, 1903, Wilbur and Orville tried to fly the *Flyer* again. Orville was the pilot. Wilbur watched from the ground. The *Flyer* took off, and it stayed up in the air for twelve seconds. That does not seem long. But it was the first flight ever for a flying machine powered by an engine.

One test flight was not enough. The brothers took turns piloting the *Flyer*. They had three more good flights. Each flight was a little bit longer than the flight before it.

Only five people watched the flights. One of the men took pictures. Orville and Wilbur studied the pictures so that they could learn from them.

Wilbur and Orville's first successful flight

What is the fifth step of the design process?

The fifth step in the design process is communicating the results. When the Wright brothers tried to communicate their results, they got a response they did not expect. They had gone to a store in Kitty Hawk to send a telegram to their father. The telegram said: "success four flights [T]hursday morning . . . started from Level with engine power alone . . ."

Wilbur and Orville asked their father to tell the newspapers about the flights. Can you guess what happened? Some newspapers didn't believe their story! No one in the world had ever flown an airplane. Were the brothers lying?

The Wright brothers sent a message to their father. They told him the good news about their successful flights.

The Wright brothers did not stop trying. They went back to Ohio and took the *Flyer* with them. They built a new workroom and made another airplane. In 1908, the brothers went to Europe for a year. They showed the people in Europe their new airplane. They flew over 200 flights in Europe. At last, people believed the brothers.

In 1914, the Franklin Institute in Philadelphia awarded a medal to the brothers. Wilbur died before they got the medal, so Orville accepted the medal for both of them. When Orville died, he gave his tools and drawings to the Institute. These items helped other airplane engineers learn more about the Wright brothers' design process.

The First Flight Monument at Kill Devil Hills honors the Wright brothers.

Do all engineers use a design process?

The Wright brothers were the first to fly an airplane with an engine. But they were not the only engineers trying to fly. Just like the Wright brothers, all engineers use a design process.

Igor Sikorsky saw a picture of the Wright brothers and their airplane. He also studied Leonardo da Vinci's drawings. Sikorsky thought he could build a helicopter.

Sikorsky's first few helicopter prototypes failed. He started designing airplanes instead. He was the first person to design a plane with more than one engine. He also designed a plane that could take off and land on water.

Sikorsky returned to his ideas about a helicopter. He tested and retested his prototype. In 1940 he flew the first helicopter. Some reporters were the first people to see it.

Sikorsky's helicopter

Other pioneers designed, tested, and built new types of aircraft. They built airships such as zeppelins. Airships stayed up in the air because they were filled with gases. But the gases made them unsafe. Airships like blimps and zeppelins were used as a means of public transportation for about 40 years. Then, an airship called the *Hindenburg* exploded in 1937. Many people died. People were afraid to travel in airships after that.

zeppelin

flying boat

Flying boats were popular in the 1920s and 1930s. These aircraft flew in the air like planes, but they landed on water. Flying boats were heavy. They were also expensive to use. Soon, seaplanes and other types of aircraft replaced them.

Tin Goose

Until the 1920s, most planes were made of wood or wood and metal. In 1927, engineers at the Ford Motor Company made the first all-metal airplane. They called it the *Tin Goose*! After that, aircraft engineers made more metal airplanes. The metal airplanes became better and safer.

What is a designed system?

A designed system is all the tools, parts, and processes that work together to achieve a goal. The bus transportation system in your city or town is a designed system. So is the water system that provides your tap water. Airplanes are used in a designed system that helps transport people and goods all over the world.

An airplane transportation system includes airplanes and airports. The terminals and runways are part of the designed system. So are the service trucks and parking lots. There are air traffic lanes in the sky. Pilots use them to fly safely from place to place. Radar shows where airplanes are in the sky. Computers keep track of schedules, passengers, and cargo. Food and other supplies are also part of the system.

airport

runway

airplane

service trucks

A designed system is a part of your designed world. The designed world is every part of your community that is designed and built by people. It includes transportation and energy systems. It also includes communication systems. Look at this chart to find out more about the parts of a designed system for airplane transportation.

Parts of a Designed System

Part	Example: Airplane Transportation System
Goal—what the system aims to do	to move cargo and passengers safely through the air from place to place
Input—what is put into the system to meet the goal	fuel for the airplane; cargo; people to ride the airplane; pilots to fly the airplane; flight attendants on the plane to take care of passengers; people on the ground to help the airplane
Processes—describe means by which the goal is to be achieved	airports, air traffic lanes, departure and arrival schedules
Output—the end product	safe and timely delivery of people and cargo
Feedback—information that tells whether or not the output is successful	records of when airplanes left and arrived

What is a technological system?

Look at the outside of a passenger jet, a large airplane. You see the body, wings, and 2 (sometimes 4) huge jet engines. The tail and rudder are at the back of the plane. The rudder helps control the plane's direction. Smaller airplanes may have one or more propellers instead of large jet engines.

All these parts of an airplane make up a technological system. A technological system is a group of tools, parts, and processes that use technology to work together.

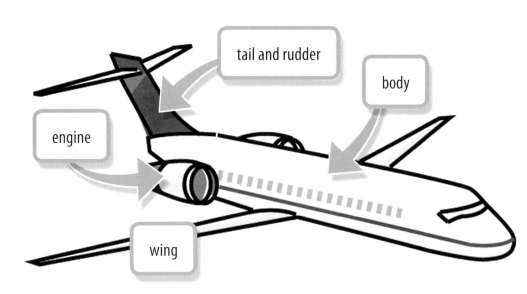

tail and rudder

body

engine

wing

Let's look inside an airplane. It is full of electronic equipment. Pilots talk to the ground crew by radio. A computer shows where the plane is located. It also shows the plane's speed as well as the weather near the plane.

An airplane has heat and air conditioning. It has lights so that passengers can see. The bathrooms have chemical toilets. Many planes have kitchens. Flight workers make coffee or heat up meals. On some airplanes, you can watch movies, play video games, or listen to music. All of these things are part of an airplane's technological system.

pilot's radio headset

flight instruments

How can the design process help you?

Now that you understand how the design process works, you can use it yourself. The design process can help you test things to see if they work. You can even test claims in advertising to see if they are true.

Imagine that you are at a toy store. You're looking for a new model glider airplane. You've seen an advertisement for a new glider. An advertisement, or ad, is an announcement a company pays for in order to sell a product. The advertisement for the new glider says that it's the fastest of all the gliders. You are not sure the claim is true. You buy the glider. At home, you use the design process to test the claim.

Step 1: You identify the problem. Is the new glider really the fastest toy glider?

You can use the design process to test claims in advertising.

Step 2: You plan and build the glider. You plan your test. You want to compare the speed with the speed of your other toy gliders. How do you do it? Design and build a test runway. Measure a section of a floor or an outdoor space. Put tape at the starting and finishing lines.

Step 3: You test the glider. You fly it and check how many seconds it takes to reach the finish line. You write the time on a chart. Then you fly all of your other gliders the same way. You record their times, too.

Glider	Time of Flight (in seconds)	Observation
Blue	13	second
Green	16	fourth
Black	15	third
New	11	fastest

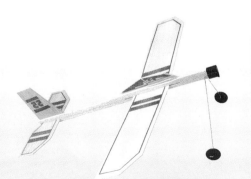

You can test each glider to find out which one flies the longest.

How do you complete the design process?

Step 4: If your first test was well designed, you don't have to redesign anything. Don't be discouraged if your test didn't work. Try it again.

Step 5: You complete the design process when you <u>communicate your results</u>. You look at the results in the chart and draw your conclusion. The new glider really is the fastest. You could send an email that describes your use of the design process to the toy company.

Now you know how the design process works. Look for more ways to use it!

Design engineers often have to try out new ways of doing things.

Improve a Design

Look around. What piece of technology in your daily life do you think you could improve? Work with a partner to brainstorm ideas. Identify a problem. What needs to be improved? Draw your ideas for a prototype on paper. Get feedback on your ideas from classmates and your teacher. Use the new ideas you get to create drawings that improve the design. Finally, draw a picture of your finished product and label its parts. With your partner, explain to the class why you think your prototype is an improvement on an existing product.

Make a Poster

Find out about someone who used the design process to invent or improve something. Use the Internet and library resources to learn about the person. Make a poster that tells about the person and what he or she invented.

Glossary

advertisement [ad•ver•tiz•muhnt] A public notice or announcement of information designed to communicate a message to a viewer or listener about a product or service. *You should use critical thinking skills to analyze the claims in an advertisement.*

design [dih• ZYN] To conceive something and prepare the plans and drawings for it to be built. *The Wright brothers worked hard to design and build an engine powered airplane.*

engineering [en•juh•NIR•ing] The application of scientific and mathematical principles to develop something practical. *The Wright brothers studied engineering to help them understand how to build their airplane.*

prototype [PROH•tuh•typ] The original or model on which something is based. *The Wright brothers built a prototype airplane.*

technology [tek•NOL•uh•jee] Any designed system, product, or process used to solve problems. *An airplane is a technology product.*

tool [TOOL] Anything used to help people shape, build, or produce things to meet their needs. *A pencil is a tool you use for writing.*